A Primary Teacher's Handbook
PE

John Davis

Acknowledgements

With thanks to the following schools:
Warmley C of E VC Primary School, South Gloucestershire and William Austin Junior School, Luton.
With thanks also to:
Anne Angus of Warmley School for her contribution to the Dance section and Ian Ward, Barbara Wilding and Phil Clarke of William Austin Junior School, Luton.
Photographs:
Sarah Davis and Peter Ryan.
Illustrations: Catherine Ward – Simon Girling and Associates.

Crown copyright is reproduced with the permission of the Controller of HMSO.

Editors: Sarah Peutrill and Andy Brown   Layout artist: Suzanne Ward   Cover design: Alison Colver/Andy Bailey
Cover images: Leah Joseph and Nabillah Patel, Uplands Junior School, Leicester

© 1997 Folens Limited, on behalf of the author.

British Library Cataloguing in Publication Data. A catalogue record for this book is available from the British Library.

First published 1997 by Folens Limited, Dunstable and Dublin.
Folens Limited, Albert House, Apex Business Centre, Boscombe Road, Dunstable, LU5 4RL, England.

ISBN 1 85276 939-4

Printed in Singapore by Craft Print.

Contents

Introduction

PE may occupy the least amount of space in the National Curriculum documentation, yet the importance of the subject in terms of the curriculum generally and in the overall development of children, both individually and collectively, should never be undervalued.

This handbook aims to provide guidance and support for the classroom teacher so that all the children in their charge receive the broad and balanced programme of PE to which they are entitled.

No attempt is made to provide a detailed scheme of work or to outline actual lesson plans. Guidance is given on suggested teaching themes and skills progression from Reception through to Year 6 in the six main areas of activity laid down in the Programme of Study. More space is devoted to Gymnastics, Games and Dance as these three have to be taught at Key Stage 1 and Key Stage 2.

This handbook could not have been produced without the help and support of teaching and non-teaching colleagues at Warmley Primary School, South Gloucestershire. Thanks are due also to the school's children who knowingly and unknowingly make their own distinctive contribution to the planning, teaching and evaluating of PE in the school.

Aims of the handbook

To support the teaching of PE by:
- ensuring good practice
- ensuring that all children, regardless of ability, gender and race receive their entitlement to the PE curriculum and the opportunity to express themselves physically in an enjoyable manner
- encouraging children to become physically active and aware of the importance of physical fitness in everyday life
- ensuring children have an understanding of the vocabulary that is used when planning, discussing, performing and evaluating physical activities
- providing children with tasks that will challenge them to make an individual response and encourage them to use good posture and develop strength, flexibility, stamina and endurance
- providing manageable problem-solving situations that will require children to question, explore and use their imagination
- enabling children to realise that initial attempts can be modified, improved and consolidated through practise and repetition
- encouraging fair play and honesty and giving children the confidence to cope with a range of outcomes including success and failure
- stressing the importance of responding to instructions and signals, following routines and observing relevant rules and codes
- developing an awareness of their own and other people's safety in a range of different environments
- promoting the importance of showing consideration for others and the value of co-operative working
- encouraging the use of appropriate footwear, clothing and protection for certain activities and the constant observation of good hygiene.

Writing a policy statement and scheme of work

All schools need to produce a whole-school policy statement and scheme of work for PE. The responsibility for doing this may lie with the curriculum co-ordinator but all documentation should be drawn up in a collaborative process by everyone involved in teaching PE in the school.

Where are we now?
Audit: use existing documents; current practices, equipment and resources; time allocation; timetabling of key areas eg hall, field and playground.

Where do we want to be?
To have a realistic, manageable and user-friendly scheme of work that allows for continuity, progression, breadth and balance; the scheme of work to be flexible and subject to regular review.

How will we know when we have arrived?
Set targets for scheme of work to be in place and operating; inform governors, parents and other interested parties.

How do we get there?
Full staff involvement and commitment; review and extension of resources; in-service practical training; use of external support (eg advisory service); planned financial allocation.

A dynamic curriculum

This is a cyclical process of development that does not stop. The starting point will always be 'Where are we now?' By the time you have reached where you wanted to be, you will be ready to ask the initial question all over again. And so the process continues.

Key elements of a PE policy statement

The purpose and meaning of PE
- What PE is and what the school aims to achieve: learning through activity, awareness and observation; developing skills and self discipline; stimulating enjoyment, satisfaction and a sense of achievement.

A balanced programme
- Give as much responsibility as possible to the children themselves. A broad, balanced programme for each key stage is laid down in the National Curriculum Programmes of Study. Work should be differentiated by task and outcome to meet the needs, ages, abilities and interests of children.

Equal opportunities
- The PE curriculum enables all children to benefit and achieve; no barrier to access or opportunity; provision for special educational needs, children more important than the activities they take part in.

PE across the curriculum
- PE makes a significant contribution to the development of cross-curricular links, especially through problem solving and decision making; assists with development of communication and numeracy skills; links with the expressive arts, eg music, drama as well as personal, health, social and safety education.

PE and Sport
- Make a clear distinction between the two: stress the essential purpose of the class-based PE lesson (see page 64).

Requirements of a PE scheme of work

A scheme of work needs to be a whole school plan. It is a working document to help teachers and children. The key words should be 'realistic', 'manageable' and 'achievable'.

Rationale for teaching each activity

The scheme of work should contain brief details of how each element in the Programme of Study makes its own distinct and unique contribution. For instance, gymnastics assists with body management and the development of good posture.

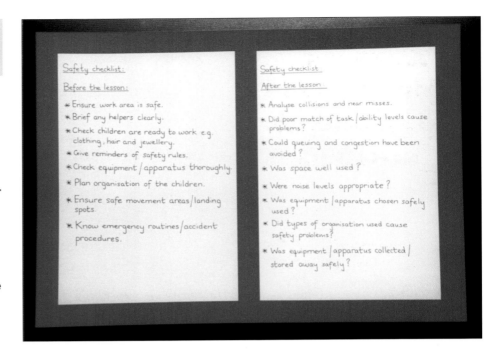

Safety checklist:

Before the lesson:

* Ensure work area is safe.
* Brief any helpers clearly.
* Check children are ready to work e.g. clothing, hair and jewellery.
* Give reminders of safety rules.
* Check equipment/apparatus thoroughly.
* Plan organisation of the children.
* Ensure safe movement areas/landing spots.
* Know emergency routines/accident procedures.

Safety checklist

After the lesson:

* Analyse collisions and near misses.
* Did poor match of task/ability levels cause problems?
* Could queuing and congestion have been avoided?
* Was space well used?
* Were noise levels appropriate?
* Was equipment/apparatus chosen safely used?
* Did types of organisation used cause safety problems?
* Was equipment/apparatus collected/stored away safely?

Framework for teaching and learning

Safety aspects Draw up ground rules for creating a safe environment; responsibilities of the teacher; safety checks before, during and after lessons; moving, using and storing apparatus and equipment.

Overall planning Choose themes in each activity; balance and breadth of each term; continuity and progression; the need for revision and repetition to allow for practice, improvement and development; details of fundamental skills; target setting for children.

Lesson planning and organisation There can be variations in lesson format but include warm up, main activity and cool down; the importance of differentiation through outcome, such as 'All throw the ball in the air and catch it', and tasks, such as one group tries ten catches with a beanbag, another with a small ball; plan the teaching points to feature in the lesson; use observation and demonstration; question children about what they are doing; always use encouragement.

Learning experiences through themes, KS1 and KS2 There should be a selection of themes (such as running with a large ball) for year groups in each key stage, with written objectives. It should include activities to carry out these themes and lists of necessary equipment and apparatus.

Resources Choose the most appropriate apparatus and equipment to suit the activity and the key stage; introduce gradually as confidence increases; check, prepare and transport apparatus and equipment; consider the safe use of inside and outside environments; book resources; use of helpers.

Assessment of children Base this on observation; determine needs of the class; pinpoint strengths and weaknesses of individual children; are objectives being achieved; children reflect on and discuss their own performances; link with National Curriculum End of Key Stage descriptions; what and when to record; reporting procedure (see page 58).

Evaluation of lessons Evaluate each session; consider enjoyment level; were tasks too easy, too hard?; were children challenged?; consider the balance between teaching and exploration; think about organisation of individuals and groups; think about suitability of equipment used (see page 61).

Review of scheme of work Get feedback from staff and children; evaluate the effectiveness of the scheme of work; amend and adapt when necessary.

A PRIMARY TEACHER'S HANDBOOK – *PE*   © Folens (not copiable)

Physical Education in the National Curriculum

General requirements

This section of the handbook provides information on what should be taught at Key Stages 1 and 2. Below are the general requirements of PE provision:

- planning
- performance
- evaluating.

The greatest emphasis should be placed on performance.

The three key elements of teaching PE are:

Physical activity

Teaching should:

- encourage children to be physically active and adopt healthy lifestyles

- encourage good posture and correct body use

- develop breathing, pulse rate, flexibility, strength and stamina

- relate personal hygiene to vigorous physical activity.

Positive attitudes

Teaching should:

- develop fair play and honest competition, good sporting behaviour in individuals, teams and spectators

- assist children to cope with success and limitations in performance

- encourage children to build up their level of competence

- help children to be mindful of others and the environment.

Safe practice

Children should be taught to:

- respond at once to instructions

- recognise and follow rules, laws, codes of etiquette and safety procedures

- use correct, safe and appropriate clothing and equipment in a range of activities

- lift, carry, place and use equipment safely

- realise the importance of warming up before exercise and recovery after it.

Programme of Study

Key Stage 1

Three areas of activity should be taught in each year of Key Stage 1. Indoor and outdoor environments should be used where appropriate.

Throughout the key stage children should be taught about changes that occur to their bodies as they exercise and to recognise the short-term effects this exercise has on the body. Swimming may be taught at Key Stage 1 if schools choose. The Programme of Study for swimming set out in Key Stage 2 should be used at the appropriate level.

Area of activity	What children should be taught
Games	Simple competitive team games – how to play them as individuals and, when ready, in pairs and small groups. How to develop and practise ways of sending, receiving and travelling with a ball, and other similar games equipment (for example throwing, catching and dribbling). Simple tactical elements of playing games including running, dodging, chasing, use of space and awareness of others.
Gymnastic activities	Different ways of performing basic actions of travelling using both hands and feet. Ways of turning, rolling, jumping, balancing, swinging and climbing using both the floor and different kinds of apparatus. Linking series of actions together into simple sequences, both on the floor and using apparatus. For example a jump, followed by a roll and then a balance.
Dance	To develop control, co-ordination, balance, poise, height in the basic actions of travelling, jumping, turning, gesture and stillness. To perform movements or patterns, some of which come from existing dance traditions, for example pat-a-cake polka. To explore moods and feelings; to develop responses to music through dance, using rhythmic responses and contrasts of speed, shape, direction and level.

Programme of Study

Key Stage 2

Six areas of activity should be taught. Games, Gymnastics and Dance should be taught each year of the key stage. Athletics, Outdoor and adventurous activities and Swimming should be taught at points during Key Stage 2. Children should also be taught about changes that occur to their bodies as they exercise, as in Key Stage 1, and to recognise the short-term effects exercise has on the body.

Area of activity	What children should be taught
Games	To understand and play small-sided games that are simple versions of recognised competitive team and individual games such as soccer, netball and cricket. Common skills and principles of games, for example attack and defence, rules and tactics. Improved skills of sending, receiving, striking and travelling with a ball in games.
Gymnastic activities	Different ways of turning, rolling, swinging, jumping, climbing, balancing, travelling on hands and feet and how to adapt, practise and refine these on floor and apparatus. To change shape, speed and direction in gymnastic actions. To practise, refine and repeat longer series of actions; make more complex movement sequences using floor and apparatus, for example sequencing three linked balances.
Dance	To compose and control movement by varying shape, size, direction, level, speed, tension and continuity, for example march with knees high. Dance forms from different times and places, including some traditional dances from the British Isles, such as the Cumberland Square Eight. To express feelings, moods and ideas, to respond to music, create characters and narratives in response to different stimuli, for example dance telling the story of *The Ugly Duckling*.

Area of activity	What children should be taught
Athletics	✋ To develop and refine basic techniques in running (for example over a short distance, in relays), throwing (for accuracy and distance) and jumping (for height and distance), using a variety of equipment. ✋ To measure, compare and improve their own performance.
Outdoor and adventurous activities	✋ To perform outdoor and adventurous activities in one or more different environments, such as the playground, school grounds and local park. ✋ To tackle challenges of a physical problem-solving nature, for example obstacle courses using suitable equipment – working as individuals and with others. ✋ To develop the skills necessary for these activities.
Swimming	✋ To swim competently, unaided and safely for at least 25 metres. ✋ To develop confidence in the water – resting, floating and supporting. ✋ To use different means of propulsion using arms and legs, developing efficient, effective strokes on front and back. ✋ The principles and skills of water safety and survival.

Planning and organising the PE lesson

Opening activity
(warm up)
Prepare the body by raising the pulse rate, improving circulation and increasing the breathing rate. The activities chosen could revise tasks done in previous lessons. You may include some element of exploration, especially for younger children. Encourage older children to devise their own routines.

Main activity
(skill development and application)
This is the core teaching part of the lesson. Introduce, practise and consolidate skills individually or in small groups. Then apply skills to problem-solving situations involving, for example, floor work and use of apparatus in gymnastics, small-sided versions of major team games, performing a dance, taking part in athletics events or swimming with a complete stroke.

Concluding activity
(cool down)
Calm and relax the body. Reflect on what has been done. Prepare the children for a return to the class. Return the pulse rate and breathing to normal. Bring mental energy under control.

The details given here will apply in general terms to lessons in Games, Gymnastics, Dance, Athletics and Swimming. Lesson planning and organising in Outdoor and adventurous activities require an amended format and this is outlined in more detail on page 48.

Health, hygiene and safety

Health and hygiene: general points

Children must change into suitable clothing for the PE lesson. Barefoot work should be encouraged on suitable indoor floor surfaces. Extra layers of clothing, such as sweatshirts, may be needed when working outside in cold weather. Teachers should be appropriately dressed, not only for ease of movement, but also to set an example.

Check floor surfaces, especially indoors to ensure that they are clean and safe. Children should ensure they have clean feet when going into a swimming pool area. They should use the shower and toilet before swimming. They should not swim after eating a large meal.

Be aware of the medical conditions of children taking part in the lesson. Essential medication, such as inhalers, should be available. If possible, let the children wash their feet after indoor floorwork.

Before the lesson

- Check the work area is safe.
- Brief any helpers on safety matters.
- Check children are ready to work safely, eg loose clothing, no jewellery.
- Remind children of safety rules.
- Check equipment and apparatus is ready and safe.
- Plan how children will be grouped and organised.
- Ensure that there are good movement areas and safe landing spots.
- Know emergency routines and accident procedures.

During the lesson

- Ensure quiet and calm entry to work area.
- Give clear and precise instructions.
- Ensure children respond immediately to instructions.
- Be well positioned to see all the children all the time.
- In swimming particularly, count heads often to ensure groups are together.
- Ensure equipment and apparatus is moved around correctly and checked before being used.
- Ensure children are aware of noise level expectations.
- Do not allow children to carry out tasks until they are given permission to do so.
- Always encourage children to handle equipment carefully.
- In games and athletics ensure hitting and throwing areas are safely positioned away from other children, obstacles and buildings.

After the lesson

- Analyse near misses and collisions.
- How can they be avoided?
- Did a poor match between task and ability cause safety problems?
- Did queuing or congested areas cause difficulties?
- Were noise levels a threat to safety?
- Was space used well overall?
- Did the choice and use of equipment and apparatus cause safety problems?
- Did class groupings aid good safety?
- Was equipment collected, checked and returned safely?

Never leave children unsupervised - good teaching is safe teaching.

A PRIMARY TEACHER'S HANDBOOK – *PE* © Folens (not copiable)

While the safety issues outlined on the previous page will apply in general terms to all PE teaching, additional specific safety matters also need to be considered when working in the areas of Athletics, Outdoor and adventurous activities and Swimming.

Athletics

- Ensure throwing areas do not interfere with other activities.
- Ensure any hurdles that are used are the correct 'knock over' type and they are facing the right way.
- If canes are used for jumping purposes, the ends should be taped. Ensure they dislodge easily.
- Long jumps with a run up should be carried out into a sand pit.
- High jumping at this level should be the foot-to-foot method. Flop style is not suitable.
- Mats can be used for high jump but they should be thick and should not move.
- Wet grass can make any athletics activities potentially dangerous.

Outdoor and adventurous activities

- Involve children in planning. Ensure (essentially for off-site visits) they are fully briefed.
- Carry out preliminary visits to the site to check routes and hazards.
- Get parental consent.
- Organise groups for the visit.
- Check school and local authority guidelines on supervision levels.
- Fully brief all helpers.
- Check insurance cover for helpers.
- Fully prepare equipment and teaching materials.
- Arrange travel.
- Check toilet arrangements.
- Check eating arrangements.
- Carry first aid and make sure there is a qualified person to use it.
- Use only fully-qualified staff for specialist activities, eg climbing and canoeing.
- Be aware of all emergency routines and accident procedures.
- Have transport backup.
- Ensure routes are well planned.
- Encourage the children to watch over each other.
- Have wet weather contingency plans.

Swimming

- Stress health, hygiene and safety matters in class preparation sessions.
- Fully brief the children on travelling routines, changing room, and poolside behaviour.
- Ensure the children and helpers are aware of emergency routines and accident procedures.
- Check the water is clear, the bottom should be clearly visible.
- Ensure qualified life-guards and resuscitators are always on the poolside.
- Encourage the children to wear hats for identification purposes. Count heads in each group frequently.
- Rope off shallow areas for beginners and less able swimmers.
- Insist on a reasonable noise level.
- Be mindful of other pool users.
- Check diving areas have the recommended depth of water.
- Ensure the equipment is stored tidily away from the poolside when not in use.
- Ensure that the children are not in the water until instructed to be so.
- Check that all the children are out of the water at the end of the session.

Storing, moving and using equipment

General guidelines

Storing

Gymnastic equipment should be kept close to the side of the hall where it can be accessed easily. Avoid storage cupboards which can become congested. With climbing frames/wall bars and so on ensure all staff know how to use and secure them. Small equipment used for games should be kept in small baskets and boxes which are easy to carry. Store on low shelves up off the floor where they are easy to get and keep tidy. Make frequent checks. The co-ordinator should be notified if items are in short supply.

Moving

Never drag equipment or lift over other items or children. Develop a correct lifting, carrying and placing system for the whole school. Train children to put out and take in apparatus as soon as possible. Teach correct methods of lifting, carrying and putting down equipment. This must be done under supervision. Never allow children to do this on their own. With younger children, some heavy items of equipment may have to be moved by the teacher. In games lessons, prepare and transport equipment to the correct location before the lesson.

Using

In Gymnastics, avoid pre-set apparatus. Avoid preconceptions by allowing each class to set up their own. Don't use items just because they are there – choose the apparatus to suit the teaching theme. Draw simple ground plans to remember where items are placed. Older children can work from these under supervision. Start younger children with small, low equipment and build up. Always check all apparatus personally before children use it. Ensure safe landing areas. Ensure ease of movement around apparatus. Avoid queues and congestion. Keep children actively involved. Reinforce safety rules. In games, ensure easy access to equipment. Send a small group at a time. Check, return and store items at the end of the lesson. Encourage tidy storing.

Equipment checklist

Schools vary considerably, but listed below are basic essential items needed to deliver the PE curriculum.

Games: Selection of balls, small, medium and large in plastic, rubber and foam; range of bats in different shapes and sizes including rounders, tennis and cricket types; hockey sticks; hoops; quoits; beanbags; ropes; canes; posts; wickets; skittles; cones; flags; braids; bibs and games tops; nets and stands; whistles; adapters; playground chalk; pump.

Gymnastic activities: Agility tables, poles, beams, trestles, planks, benches, mats, climbing frame; stage sections; bar box (detachable top).

Dance: Visual, auditory and tactile stimuli, eg objects, pictures, designs and props; written resources, eg poems; CDs and tapes; CD/tape player with speakers; percussion instruments.

Athletics: As Games above, plus tape-measures; stop-watches; recording equipment including clipboards, pens and so on.

Swimming: Floats, armbands and other floatation aids; rope pool dividers; objects to pick up from bottom of pool; objects to blow across surface; hoops; balls, buckets, ropes and so on for rescue work.

Outdoor and adventurous activities: Maps; flags; tapes; control markers; compasses; recording equipment; adult helpers and supervisors.

Storing, moving and using equipment

One child at each corner. Lift, never drag. Thumbs on top, fingers underneath. Lift with back straight and carry sideways.

Two carriers, facing each other. Travel sideways or, if not possible, look over shoulder.

Two carriers, one each side. Move sideways.

Four carriers, one in each corner. Move forwards.

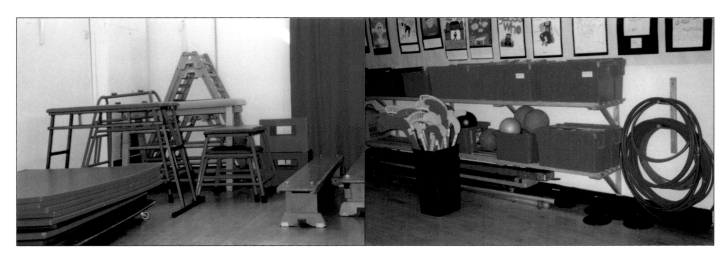

Close to the walls for ease of movement. Avoid awkward store-rooms.

Off the floor for easy storage. Low shelves so it is easy to lift and move containers.

A PRIMARY TEACHER'S HANDBOOK – *PE*

Games

Games permit children to develop their own level of expertise in the basic skills. They increase children's knowledge and understanding of major games and aid their social development, helping them to lead and be led in co-operative situations. Games help children's thinking, problem-solving and decision-making skills.

What to teach

Skill development (see below).

Principles of play and tactics such as attack/defence rules.

Designing and making own games. This is linked to the two areas above and should not be seen in isolation.

Types of games

Invasion games such as football, rugby, netball and hockey. Think about attack, defence, possession, shooting.

Net and racket games such as tennis, volley ball, badminton. Think about sending, receiving, positional play, serving.

Strike and field games such as rounders, cricket, softball. Think about batting, bowling, fielding, making runs.

Basic skills

Sending
Think about direction, distance, weight, release, follow through.

Receiving
Think about flight, body, position, give.

Travelling
With and without the ball. Think about control, speed, direction.

Developing skills and understanding through themes

A selection of teaching themes for games are given in the next section. Details are given as to how these themes can be taught progressively from Reception through to Year 6. This progression is presented as a guide only. It is important to remember that progression is not always linear and that any child could be working on a number of different stages at any one time. The photographs and illustrations emphasise teaching points that can be made during the teaching of these themes.

Progression through Games

Walks, runs, hops, skips, jumps and stops on command.

Plays follow-my-leader games, uses space, shows awareness of others and can walk in straight lines.

Follows straight, curved and zigzagged pathways and relay runs. Negotiates obstacles.

Travelling (no ball)

Reception

Moves forwards, backwards and sideways, quickly stopping and starting.

Plays simple tag games and runs, dodges, avoids and catches.

Works in pairs, following, dodging and weaving in a confined space.

Changes direction and links changes in speed with quick turns and safe footwork.

Controls speed while sprinting, walking and jogging using stride length and arms and making fast starts.

Feints and dodges, getting away from a marker.

Marks a partner, closing down and anticipating angle and speed of pass.

Year 6

Travelling (with ball)

Reception →

Bounces a large ball on the spot with two hands, progressing to one. →

Bounces a large ball at waist height on the spot. Uses one hand and pushes down with spread fingers.

↓

Bounces a large ball while moving at a slow pace, avoiding obstacles.

↓

Travels with a ball and hockey stick, can watch feet and change speed and direction. ←

Bounces a large ball, around obstacles with control, shields opponent. ←

Bounces a ball with increased speed, stopping, starting and changing direction.

↓

Controls a large ball at feet and moves around, changing speed and direction.

↓

Carries a rugby ball, point down with spread hands around it and times passes.

↓

Controls a ball closely with hands or feet in opposed situations and pairs. →

Travels with a ball with hands or feet in small games activities and scores goals or points. →

Year 6

Sending large ball (with hands)

Holds a ball with two hands, bouncing and catching and cradling it to the body.

Rolls a ball, runs, overtakes and crouches to receive.

Bounces a ball on the spot, at the side of the body with stronger hand and spread fingers.

Passes to a partner from the chest, with two hands, fingers spread around the ball.

Bounces to the chest of a partner, works on strength and accuracy.

Passes from chest with receiver showing where ball should go and moving to the space.

Holds a rugby ball with hands spread and passes it, swinging arms across the body.

Passes with a straight arm from the shoulder, one hand supporting, the other pushing through.

Passes overhead (above, not behind head). Is able to volley and dig the ball.

Aims at targets such as a netball net at a low height.

Reception

Year 6

Sending small ball (with hands)

Throws a beanbag, underarm up in the air and catches at a low height.

→

Throws and catches a beanbag at short distances, in pairs; works on direction and weight.

→

Throws a beanbag underarm, in pairs, into a hoop on the ground. Bounces a small ball through a hoop to a partner.

Reception

Throws a small ball, in pairs, through a hoop held by a third child. Works on direction and accuracy.

Rolls a ball to a partner, along the ground between targets; gap narrowed progressively.

Throws underarm to a partner and follows through, moving legs to balance.

Throws underarm at a target such as a container, varying targets and distances.

Fields a ball in a game and returns to target or team mate.

Aims and throws at various targets such as canes, skittles and wickets.

Throws overarm with arm back, pulling through, working on grip and direction.

Year 6

A PRIMARY TEACHER'S HANDBOOK – PE

Sending large ball (with feet)

Explores kicking a large ball with different parts of the feet.

→

Passes a ball along the ground using the strongest foot and stopping each time.

→

Passes with side of foot, stops, returns and passes back aiming for accuracy and correct weighting.

Reception

Passes with side of foot and kicks directly, aiming at targets, such as cones or skittles.

Passes with the instep between a target in pairs, keeping control; narrows the targets.

←

Passes with the instep, head over ball and non-striking foot alongside; stops ball each time.

Passes the ball in the air and with the instep chips to a partner; hits the ball in the lower half, body leans back.

Year 6

Passes ball and moves into space, judges weight, link control.

Receives a pass and scores a goal against a goalkeeper, aiming low and keeping to the corners.

←

Hits targets such as cones, flags, stationary balls at varying distances; works in pairs.

Receiving a ball (with hands)

Throws and catches a beanbag by watching, spreading hands and grasping.

→

Bounces a large ball and catches with two hands, bringing to body.

→

Throws a beanbag in the air and catches with two hands by reaching and cradling.

↓

Reception

Moves into position to receive a ball and gets body in line.

←

Throws a ball in the air to a partner who rolls it back. Later the tasks are switched.

←

Throws a small ball underarm to a partner who catches it on the bounce.

↓

Watches ball from partner's hand and improves shape of cradle.

↓

Catches from overarm throw having watched the flight of the ball.

↓

Gets body in line to receive the ball from the field, air, ground and bounce.

→

Fields ball and returns to target, has positional sense and anticipates the shot.

→

Year 6

A PRIMARY TEACHER'S HANDBOOK – *PE*

Striking a ball (hitting)

Reception ➡️ Develops hand/eye co-ordination; throws a beanbag in the air, moves hand and lets it hit. ➡️ Uses palm of hand to bat away a small ball that is in the air.

⬇️

Bounces a ball continuously on the floor with hand at waist height.

⬇️

Keeps a ball up in the air as long as possible using various bats. ⬅️ Throws underarm to partner who hits back, keeping the distance short. ⬅️ Uses a small bat to keep ball bouncing, in the air.

⬇️

Passes a ball in pairs with a two-sided (unihoc) hockey stick, checking hand grip.

⬇️

Passes a ball to a partner with control and accuracy, not trying to beat opponent.

⬇️

Passes a ball over line or net to a partner, with a bounce before return. ➡️ Plays bat and ball activities involving serve and return to beat opponents. ➡️ **Year 6**

Designing own games

Reception

→ Individuals make slight changes to games already played, eg throw a beanbag underarm through a small hoop, instead of large hoop.

→ Individual children set targets for themselves, eg successively catching a beanbag six times.

↓

Individual children are given the equipment to be used and decide on the game themselves, eg using a tennis racket to keep a ball in the air.

↓

Pairs game: children work together to reach a set target, eg one throws a ball, the other bats it into a target area.

↓

Pairs game: children oppose each other, eg within a 10m grid one child rolls a ball along the ground to get it past a partner.

↓

Devises tag games for small groups (5–6), eg one has to catch the others or remove a 'tail' from the others' shorts. Each child explains the rules to the others.

← Small groups devise games needing a pitch or restricted area, eg 10m grids.

← Designs games for a group with a scoring system, points or goals.

↓

Designs games with emphasis on tactics and breaking down the opposition.

→ Designs games with agreed rules, decides sanctions for breaking rules and shares refereeing duties.

→ **Year 6**

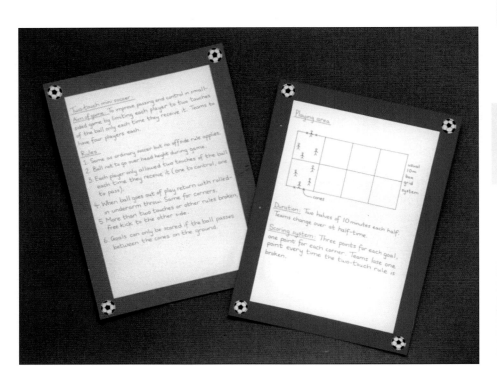

A PRIMARY TEACHER'S HANDBOOK – *PE*

Gymnastics

In addition to being an enjoyable sport, gymnastic activities:

- help children to develop an understanding of not only how their bodies move but how this movement can be managed
- develop strength, fitness and flexibility and promote physical skills
- encourage creativity and the use of imagination and foster attitudes of courage and perseverance
- present children with challenging problem-solving tasks that have to be solved.

What to teach

Floor and apparatus work

- Ways of travelling using hands and feet. These include turning, jumping, swinging, rolling, climbing and balancing.

- Changes in shape, speed and direction (especially Key Stage 2).

- Linking the above movements with simple joined actions through to more complex sequences.

Developing skills and understanding through themes

Units of work in gymnastic activities are based on specific aspects of movement. These are best taught through themes. A selection of themes are given in the following section, with an outline of how they can be progressively taught from Reception through to Year 6. This progression is presented as a guide only. It is important to remember that progression is not always linear and that any child could be working on a number of different stages at any one time. The photographs emphasise teaching points that can be made during the teaching of these themes. In gymnastics, a basic strategy might be: select a theme, introduce the theme, develop the theme, extend the theme (sometimes using apparatus). Movement should be analysed in terms of what is happening, how it is happening, where it is happening and with whom it is happening.

Progression through Gymnastics

Walks alone, following the teacher or others.

→ Uses available space, walks, runs and steps on command.

↑

Use of space   **Reception**

↓

Travels with small and big steps.

↓

Travels over floor, using hands and feet. ← Travels backwards, forwards, sideways and changes direction. ← Travels by bouncing, hopping, skipping and jumping.

↓

Travels over small apparatus, such as benches and mats, jumping off safely. → Uses other body parts to move over apparatus, sliding, curling and stretching. → Changes levels, speed and direction on apparatus.

↓

Sequences forms of travelling on floor and apparatus.

↓

Year 6

Body shape

Changes body shape on feet, eg tall, fat, stretching parts out and bringing parts in.

Changes body shape at floor level, as before.

Moves from one body shape to another, with control, eg tight curl to long thin stretch.

Reception

Finds different parts of the body to curl and change shape.

Moves over low apparatus, eg benches and mats, using different body shapes.

Moves over large apparatus, eg boxes or climbing frame, curling, stretching and changing body shape.

Takes body weight on hands, moves legs and feet into different shapes.

Jumps from apparatus, making shapes in the air and landing safely.

From balanced positions, stretches in different directions to show new shape.

Moves over apparatus in pairs, showing different body shapes, one leading, one following.

Year 6

Supporting body weight

Reception

With weight on feet, lowers and touches the floor and other parts of the body lightly.

Jumps, lands on two feet, lowers to the ground and rolls.

Curls up, rolls, stops and balances and uses different body parts.

Balances on different parts of the body, eg hands, feet and shoulders.

Balances on small apparatus, such as planks and benches.

Hangs from an apparatus, (eg a climbing frame), using different parts of the body, (eg hands and backs of knees).

Balances on apparatus, using patches (large body parts) and points (small body parts).

Year 6

Follows and copies partner over apparatus as they support bodyweight in different ways.

Links floor sequences of patch and point balances smoothly.

Travels across and through apparatus, eg benches and agility tables, and takes the weight on patches and points.

A PRIMARY TEACHER'S HANDBOOK – *PE*

Transferring body weight

Finds different ways of travelling on feet, eg two on to one, two on to two. →

Stands and lowers to floor and rocks back to feet. →

Controls a series of balance positions, working through a sequence.

↓

Moves continuously on the floor and brings as many body parts into contact as possible.

↓

As above over small apparatus, eg mats and benches.

↓

Moves from floor to apparatus and back again, transferring weight on to different body parts.

↓

Reception

↑

Finds ways of getting on to and leaving apparatus using different body parts. ←

Makes up a floor sequence that shows moving on feet, rolls and balances. ←

Travels on small apparatus, using body parts other than hands and feet.

↓

Works in pairs on apparatus, transferring bodyweight shows changes alternating between speed and direction.

↓

Year 6

Flight

Runs and leaps into the air off one foot and lands on two feet.

→

Revises different jumping movements over the floor, working on safe landings.

→

Jumps to show different body shapes in the air, eg thin and wide.

↓

Jumps to show turns in the air, using arms to gain extra height.

↓

Links jumps with other movements, eg balances and rolls; makes up simple sequences.

←

Jumps from small apparatus, eg benches and boxes, pushing up for height.

←

Finds ways on to apparatus using a leap or jump.

↑

Reception

↓

Jumps on to apparatus and jumps off showing body shapes in flight.

↓

With a partner, works out a routine of jumps and in-flight shapes on the floor.

↓

With a partner, works out a routine of jumps on selected apparatus and jumps over partner on the floor.

↓

Year 6

A PRIMARY TEACHER'S HANDBOOK – *PE*

Levels and directions

Jumps and stretches to reach high levels; crouches and bends to reach low levels.

Balances on different body parts as near to the floor as possible and stretches away as far as possible.

Revises ways of moving forwards, sideways and up and down, using different parts of the body.

Finds ways of moving on hands and feet, keeping close to the floor then reaching as high as possible.

Reception

Creates a pattern of jumps that takes the body in different directions.

Moves over apparatus to show contrasts, eg high to low, low to high.

Gets on apparatus forwards and leaves sideways, backwards or diagonally.

Travels on benches, planks and beams at both low and high levels.

Creates a floor sequence – shows contrast between moving in at least two directions.

Creates a sequence with a partner that shows contrasts in levels and changes in direction.

Year 6

Partner/small group work

Has a good repertoire of individual movements, such as rolls, balances and jumps.

→

Static copying tasks: one matches the other; takes turns to be the leader.

→

Follows the leader over floor-based moves, eg jumping; stresses smooth movements.

↓

Follows the leader on small apparatus, eg benches and tables; the leader demonstrates several times.

↓

Contrasts tasks on floor showing differences in timing and shape, eg quick, slow, curl and stretch.

↓

As above on small apparatus showing extremes, eg high and low, rounded and thin.

←

Over/under theme: makes a still obstacle and partner passes over or under, not touching.

←

Pairs support each other in contact, eg help keep balance.

↓

Works in groups of three to four and follows leader, matching moves; the last person could contrast the moves.

↓

Works in groups of three to four, supporting each other, eg aiding balance.

↓

Reception

Year 6

A PRIMARY TEACHER'S HANDBOOK – *PE*

Using apparatus

Uses floor space well, avoids queues and congestion.

→

Uses floor space well when the apparatus is out.

→

Applies safety rules, eg stops, comes off the apparatus and sits on the floor.

↓

Reception

Moves well from the floor to the apparatus and vice versa.

↓

Uses all the apparatus available; finds different starting points.

↓

Moves with control over apparatus, eg forwards and backwards.

←

Finds a holding position and balances with control on apparatus.

←

Gets on and off a greater range of apparatus, eg wall bars and climbing frames.

↓

Works in pairs on apparatus, especially follow-the-leader and matching tasks.

↓

Carries out small group work, eg contrasting each other's moves and over and under tasks.

→

Year 6

Dance

Dance enables children to:

- communicate meaning in a non-verbal way
- acquire and develop performing skills, especially those that focus on expressive qualities or movement
- compose their ideas and feelings though movement
- share and participate in traditional and social dance forms.

What to teach

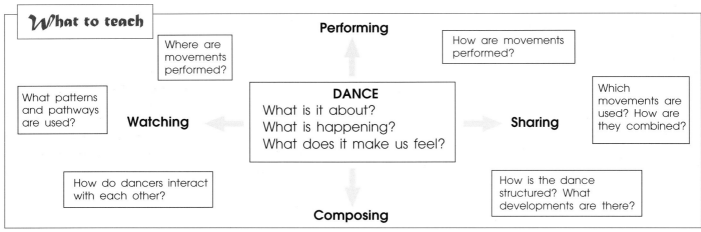

Performing

Where are movements performed?

How are movements performed?

What patterns and pathways are used?

Watching

DANCE
What is it about?
What is happening?
What does it make us feel?

Sharing

Which movements are used? How are they combined?

How do dancers interact with each other?

How is the dance structured? What developments are there?

Composing

Developing skills and understanding through themes

Dance involves combining different movements and performing them in such a way that meaning is communicated. It differs from the other aspects of PE (Games and Gymnastic activities) because, although involving similar skills and agilities, the quality and manner of movement evoke meaning and atmosphere. It is non-verbal communication. Children may run to catch a ball and run before a jump but in dance that run is performed in such a way that, for example, the movement of a bird is suggested.

Through experiencing and participating in dance, children will build up an awareness of types of movements, ways of moving and where they are in space and in relation to others. They will learn to structure and compose dances using different choreographic elements. They will respond to a wide variety of stimuli and react to the rhythm and mood of different music.

The different themes in dance all interact together. In separating them out it is hoped to show the gradual progression of skill that can be developed in the children so that they become accomplished performers and composers.

This progression is presented as a guide only. It is important to remember that progression is not always linear and that any child could be working on a number of different stages at any one time. The photographs emphasise teaching points that can be made during the teaching of these themes.

Progression through Dance

Awareness of body parts, eg rub feet, and isolated movement, eg shrug shoulders.

→ Increases pulse rate by racing, walking, skipping, hopping and running.

Starting activities

Reception

Stretches on the floor to help maintain balance and support movement.

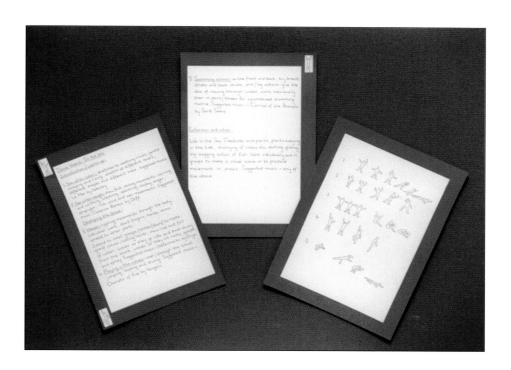

Structures simple repetitive and continuous movement, eg eight walks, eight runs followed by four jumps.

Moves more specific individual body parts and whole body, eg swinging actions to improve suppleness and flexibility.

Reviews dance plans and notes, discusses and evaluates work to enhance and improve quality.

Explores stimulus through discussion before session begins and talks about previous work before continuing.

Plans independent warm-up activities, showing an awareness of purpose and safety.

Combines two or three warm-up activities into sequences that can be repeated, eg eight arm swings and four shoulder shrugs.

Begins to understand the effect warm-up activities have on the body, eg stretch of muscles and increase of pulse rate.

Year 6

Making up a dance

Reception

Experiences dances with a clear beginning and end, eg teacher suggests all start with a bow and then end on the floor waving legs and arms.

Combines elements where there is a structure, eg skips around in a circle with improvised sections, makes up juggling movements.

Improvises in response to a stimulus and music, eg a clown or a swan.

Develops rhythmic responses and clear phrases of movement, eg stamps foot to a rhythm.

Begins to create simple dance sequences and forms these into simple structures guided by the teacher.

Selects travelling movements such as turns and jumps to suggest meaning and establish moods, eg anger or a particular character such as a train passenger.

Creates own movement, eg stamps feet and shakes fists, then runs forward and stamps feet, circling to suggest anger.

Works co-operatively with partners and small groups to perform their own dances, remembering the movement sequences and overall form.

Structures are increasingly complex, eg repeating one part of a chorus with variations on one theme between.

Year 6

Creates dances with good beginnings, developments and contrasts and strong endings, with less teacher guidance.

Develops and extends movement phases by using repetition in a contrasting way, eg changing speed, shape, direction or level.

A PRIMARY TEACHER'S HANDBOOK – *PE*

Moods, characters and stories

Reception

Uses words as a stimulus for dance, eg stretch, explode and drop, and nursery rhymes, such as *Jack and Jill* and *Humpty Dumpty*.

Uses pictures or objects as a stimulus for a dance as something or someone, eg a caterpillar or a balloon.

Responds to music that strongly suggests moods and feelings, eg happiness, anger, fear, sadness.

Uses body shapes and ways of moving that associate with the mood or feeling being explored, eg bouncy and jerky movements suggesting happiness.

Beginning and ending movements are used to suggest an idea or action, eg all toys jump in a box.

Creates simple characters by using movement phrases, eg a leap, two strides and a lunge for an 'invader' coming ashore.

Feelings, moods and ideas become more subtle and complex, eg sinister movements – lots of pauses, creeping and sudden jerkiness.

Follows a story-line for all or part of the dance, eg tells the story of Daedalus and Icarus in a dance.

Takes an aspect of a story and explores and extends the action in a more interpretative manner, eg exhilaration in the flight of Daedalus and Icarus and the grief that surrounds the fall.

Movements become less literal and represent ideas in a suggestive and expressive way.

Year 6

Stillness and gesture

Reception

Moves just one body part, eg head, from side to side, swings an arm from the elbow. Develops movements into gestures that fit the dance stimulus.

Responds to a command to freeze the action in a given shape or pose. Starts by copying the teacher and then thinks of own pose, eg angry, happy, like a clown or robot.

Uses pictures and photographs as a stimulus for poses that create an image, eg swans. Uses different body shapes to imitate and interpret the picture.

Stands absolutely still and holds for a count of three before moving on. This teaches control and can hold the attention of the audience.

Works in pairs, views and then copies the partner's pose. Develops an appreciation of how their body shapes appear to others and if their movement is being interpreted as they intend.

Using the pictures that are most successful, refines the movements and then selects the best ideas to include in a dance.

Links movements out of and into a 'frozen' position. Holds the moment of stillness and then flows out of it.

Creates tableau pictures where the individuals are part of the whole picture. Uses dancers at different levels and uses this frozen moment as a beginning, end or focus point in the dance.

Works in pairs, linking together using different body parts. Creates tension and contrast between the two, eg high, low, soft and strong.

Uses gestures, like the flick of the wrist, salute of the arm and roll of the hands to build up the characterisation within a dance. Repeats them in an exaggerated manner, slowly and quickly.

Year 6

A PRIMARY TEACHER'S HANDBOOK – *PE*

Travelling

Reception

Walks in own pathways, stopping at a command. Walks in time to a percussion rhythm and stops when it stops. It can get faster and slower.

↓ →

Skips, hops and gallops with a side-stepping action. Moves on the spot and across the space. Listens to the rhythm and responds, eg on the spot for four counts and across the space for eight counts.

→

Imitates animal movements using different parts of the body in contact with the floor. Creeps, crawls and scuttles like a snake, snail and lizard. Glides, hovers, swoops like a bird. Chooses two movements and repeats.

↑

Runs lightly, darting, plodding and jogging. Responds to teaching points, such as 'Up on the balls of your feet, head or chest leading the way.'

↓

Puts different travelling steps into a simple sequence, following teacher commands or percussion cues, eg walks for four counts, stands on the spot and claps for four, steps and hops turning on the spot for eight counts and then repeats.

↓

Introduces jumps and turns into travelling sequences, two feet to two feet, leaping. Takes off from a run, makes a strong shape in the air and lands carefully, continuing the forward motion.

↓

Repeats simple sequences of travelling steps, introducing contrasting speeds and levels, eg starts slowly and repeats quickly, lightly and then strongly.

↓

Performs more complex and sustained step patterns, with accompanying head and arm gestures.

← Increases the complexity of step patterns incorporating turns, eg three steps and a hop, three steps and a clap, while turning to the right and then turning to the left.

← Creates sequences of movements in response to word prompts – glides, darts and creeps. Uses isolated body parts, eg head, arms and hands to enrich the movement.

↓

Year 6

Patterns and pathways

Reception

Moves in diagonals from corner to corner. Follows the leader moving as a whole class to cross the space.

Creates other patterns moving around the floor, incorporating straight lines and curves. Moves in large and small circles and spirals and zigzags.

Finds a space to work, shows an awareness of where the other children are; stretches out arms to find own space.

Explores different ways of moving away from and towards this spot; up and down, forwards and backwards and from side to side. Makes some movements small and others large.

Varies the level of movement, sometimes high and sometimes low, developing contrasts between the two.

Puts together simple sequences of movement that follow set pathways, eg comes forwards, then retreats, then moves in a large circle; repeats the sequence but reverses the direction.

Draws a pathway on paper and then interprets this in movements. Teaches it to a partner and then performs it with partners.

Uses a variety of contrasting pathways and patterns that link with the theme of the dance, eg a dance on trains uses lots of circle patterns to associate with wheels.

Stages a dance that shows an awareness of the direction of the audience. Makes effective use of all available space, eg not all huddled in one corner.

Uses a wider variety of levels, between high, medium and low.

Uses floor patterns that are more complex with dancers working as a group weaving in and out of each other and crossing over.

Year 6

A PRIMARY TEACHER'S HANDBOOK – *PE*

𝒟ancing with others

Dances in a group, eg follows teacher in pathways, walks round and comes into the middle of a circle.

Joins with a partner or small group and follows the leader, copies movements exactly, then changes leader.

Half the class performs movement phrases and the other half responds – a question-and-answer pattern.

Performs around a stationary partner, then changes over.

Travels away from and back to partner, links arms and moves with partner.

The movements and shapes of one dancer or group are complemented by the partner of another group, eg perform spirals but at different levels.

Teaches a movement phrase to a partner, who then extends it.

In groups, performs movements in canon: dancer A starts, B joins in after A completes a phrase, C joins in after B has completed a phrase and so on.

Keeps to a place in group patterns and formations, eg circles, spirals and lines.

Creates and performs dances as individuals, in pairs and in small or large groups using a full range of choreographic elements.

𝒴ear 6

A PRIMARY TEACHER'S HANDBOOK – *PE*

Steps for folk dance

Reception

Claps hands, stamps feet and clicks fingers in time to the music to feel the beat.

→

Skips around in a circle for 16 beats and then stops. Learns to listen to calls and responds while dancing.

→

Works in pairs, clapping hands together. Performs right- and left-hand turns. Pairs hold hands and turn each other around.

→

Promenades where the pairs cross hands and then skip around the circle following the pair in front.

Puts together simple sequences using these movements and responds to calls following traditional dances.

Learns to do-se-do. Faces partner and takes three steps forward and one step to the side to go behind the partner, then four steps backwards to return to place.

Performs right- and left-hand stars when dancing in sets. Four children join hands in the centre and skip around in a circle. Each pair has to find the pair to dance with in time.

Performs dances where the whole class works together using more complex figures. Puts together figures in their own dances.

Performs a grand chain. In a circle partners face each other and give right hands. Moves forward past partners, giving left hand to the next person and so on, following the call.

In sets, learn to cast off: the children in one line follow the leader in a circle back to the bottom of the set. Dancers have to follow, remember moves and keep time.

Year 6

Athletics

Athletics encourages children to:

- compete against themselves and others
- develop their speed, strength and stamina
- take part in and manage a competition
- go further, faster and higher.

What to teach

Develop skills in measuring, timing, judging and recording. Measure, compare and improve performance in three linked areas:

- **Running and walking**
  Individually and in teams. Speed work and non-competitive longer runs.

- **Jumping**
  For accuracy, height and distance.

- **Throwing**
  For accuracy and distance. Concentrate on push (like a shot-put action), pull (like a javelin action) and sling (like a discus action).

There will be occasions when working in athletics will involve a combination of these activities. Hurdling, for example, includes both running and jumping and the approach to some throwing events may require a run up. Opportunities should be given for children to devise their own events and mini-competitions. These could include trying to beat their own best performance, trying to attain set standards or competing against other children.

Developing skills and understanding through themes

Athletics is not a statutory requirement for teachers in Key Stage 1. There is, however, much learning potential here and it would seem sensible that younger children are introduced to as many of the basic skills as teachers think appropriate. Groundwork laid down in Key Stage 1 will enhance the quality of work shown in Key Stage 2.

The main teaching themes for athletics are given on the next pages. Details are also given as to how these themes can be taught progressively from Reception through to Year 6. This progression is presented as a guide only. It is important to remember that progression is not always linear and that any child could be working on a number of different stages at any one time. The photographs emphasise teaching points that can be made during the teaching of these themes.

Progression through Athletics

Runs on the spot, checks balls of the feet, knee lifts and the position of arms.

→

Revises short runs, stops and starts on command and checks reaction times.

↓

Reception

Runs forward (10m), starts on 'go', stressing push away.

↓

Changes pace; walking, jogging, sprinting, building up speed and slowing down.

↓

In groups, jogging; back runner sprints to front of line.

↓

Runs as far as can in set time, eg two minutes.

↓

Sustains running, checks balance, strides and breathing rate. Maximum distance 800–1000m.

←

Works on correct finish by sustaining run and leaning torso forward to cross the line.

↑

Works on correct standing start – toe on the line, leans forward, arms ready.

←

Sprints over marked course, squares, slalom and so on, maximum distance 60–80m.

Year 6

A PRIMARY TEACHER'S HANDBOOK – *PE*

Running in groups (relays)

Plays tag-chasing games, eg chases others to remove braid from back of shorts.

→ Completes individual shuttle runs with short, straight distances between markers.

→ Completes shuttle runs in pairs, touches hands for change over.

Reception

Completes shuttle runs with varying courses, eg slaloms and square circuits.

Completes shuttle runs in small teams of three to four; counts the runs made in 30 seconds or a minute.

Passes an object, such as a beanbag at the end of each shuttle run.

Runs baton relays, facing each other, right hand to right hand.

Exchanges baton relays from behind; walks then jogs, then goes left hand to right hand.

Runs a baton relay at pace with restricted take-over area.

Year 6

Jumping (distance/height)

Reception

Uses spread ropes or marked lines; jumps from a standing start, crouches and springs using arms. →

Measures partner's height on the floor and attempts to jump this length.

↓ (from Reception)

↓ (to Measures)

↑ (to Uses spread ropes)

Bounces on the spot with two feet, pushes up, uses arms to gain height. →

Revises other jumps, eg one foot to one foot and one foot to two.

Uses hoops to aid combination jumps, eg three hops, three steps – chooses best take-off foot.

Works on two-footed long jumps, works on safe landing and avoids toppling back.

Makes small jumps from a standing start, tries to get over obstacles. ←

Stands on bench, arm outstretched with other child jumping to touch. ←

Makes up own combination jumps, eg step, hop and leap, step.

Combines running and jumping over obstacles at varying heights.

Year 6

A PRIMARY TEACHER'S HANDBOOK – *PE*

Throwing
(push, pull, sling action)

Reception

Tries out ways of throwing using a variety of equipment; works on accuracy and distance.

Throws a large ball with a two-handed push from chest, to hit a target; sitting, kneeling and standing.

Throws one-handed from the shoulder, aiming a small ball at a bin; sitting, kneeling and standing.

As the last stage, with increased distance and throwing over an obstacle, eg pile of cones.

Throws a small ball at targets, eg wickets and skittles; sitting, kneeling and standing.

Pull throws at a distance using lines, aiming at zones or aiming for a cross.

Pull throws with a run up. Takes arm back before, follows through after and side on.

Sling throws a large ball overhead, soccer style; sitting, kneeling and standing.

Sling throws a quoit or a ball in a sock, draws back and follows through; sitting, kneeling and standing.

Plays mini-competitions in groups, with throwing activities, points and a scoring system.

Year 6

Outdoor and adventurous activities

Outdoor activities enable children to:

- discover, explore and develop their spirit of adventure
- work in the context of practical situations and interactive relationships
- make decisions not only affecting themselves but also other people
- understand more about a range of different environments.

What to teach

Teach key skills in:

- **using maps**
- **orienteering**
- **problem solving**.

In all three areas use a range of locations starting with the more familiar such as school buildings and move to those away from the school such as the local park, woodland, riverside and sea-shore.

In this area of the PE curriculum there will be strong links with both geography and mathematics. Special consideration needs to be given to safety in outdoor and adventurous activities, especially for events that take place off school premises. In planning activities, teachers should consult DFE publications on safety in outdoor pursuits and local authority guidelines. See also page 13 for issues to think about. On page 63 a copy of a sample letter is given for those wishing to take children out of school.

Developing skills and understanding through themes

As in previous sections, skills progression is outlined in the three main areas – using maps, orienteering and problem solving. Details are also given of how to use different locations progressively as children develop their skills.

The progression shown is only a guide. It is important to remember that progression is not always linear and that any child could be working on a number of different stages at any one time. The photographs emphasise teaching points that can be made during the teaching of these themes.

Much introductory work, especially in using maps, can be class based. Lesson organisation should follow a five-stage plan: set up the activity, introduce and discuss it, carry it out, review and evaluate and, finally, plan the next stage forward.

Progression through Outdoor and adventurous activities

Teacher shows and discusses with the children examples of simple maps and plans.

Are introduced to drawings of simple objects, side and plan views.

Using maps

Reception

Sketches maps of classroom and rooms at home, locates own places.

Uses school plan, finds routes around the classes and discusses right and left turns.

Devises routes around apparatus on hall floor, drawing plans for others to follow.

Introduced to map orientation, moving map to face the way they are going.

Uses grids to show location, eg children in rows.

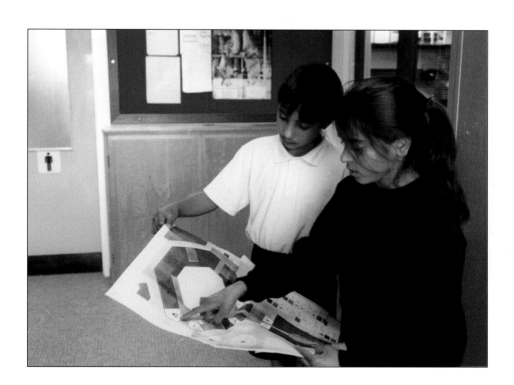

Works out a compass direction from a fixed spot, eg 'the hall is south of me'.

Has an idea of scale when comparing routes. Can decide which way is shorter.

Uses grids, scales and compass directions to devise trails in school or in outside environments.

Year 6

Orienteering

Reception

Extends to hall or playground, with a sticker to collect from each location found. → Locates fixed points on a map of the school grounds.

Revises work done on simple maps, checks use of symbols. → Locates items in the classroom on a trail, eg find four red boxes.

Matching trail task: each child has a card with numbers on it. Each stopping point on the trail indicates a letter that goes with its number, eg C goes with 5; this is used to prove that the children have been to every point.

Star activity: returns to base each time for map of new location.

Hare and hounds; follows trail left by others, introduces dead ends.

Distance walks between controls. Given distance and direction of next location.

Year 6

Teams of four to five children choose who does what and in which order. Introduce time restrictions. ← Walks a compass trail with each control giving a new direction for children to follow.

A PRIMARY TEACHER'S HANDBOOK – *PE*

Problem solving

Reception

Builds simple obstacles in pairs, given simple equipment.

→

Devises obstacle courses in pairs, for each to try.

↑

Makes a new course in pairs and draws a plan for another pair to make.

→

Lists items to gather with a partner, eg piece of wood or something red.

↓

Works in small teams with human resources only, gets one child over a gap without touching the floor.

↓

Builds a bridge using equipment such as ropes, planks and benches.

←

Works in small teams with one 'sighted' member only, steering the blindfolded others through the course.

←

Works in teams in a small confined area; changes places without stepping outside.

↓

Rescues objects from no-go areas, working as a team.

↓

Over rough ground, such as a park, woodland and moorland, finds materials in the environment that can be used to transport a small item, without touching it.

↓

Year 6

Using the environment

Reception

Arranges items on a table, changes seats and views from different positions.

Moves around areas within the classroom and is aware of own place in relation to others.

Uses the areas immediately around the classroom, eg corridors, cloakroom entrances and exits, making safe movements.

Moves to other rooms in the school building, eg hall and cooking area. Works on which routes to follow.

Utilises playground and field, eg trees, pitch areas, surveys and trails.

Goes hill walking and rock climbing in a rough terrain area, obeying the country code.

Creates surveys of water-based routes: rivers, lakes, coastal paths and beaches.

Utilises footpaths, roads around the school, building surveys and uses the Green Cross Code.

Creates a survey of a woodland area, looking at conservation, wildlife habitats and nature trails.

Creates surveys of the local park, trees, play areas and ponds.

Year 6

Swimming

Swimming:
- promotes health and fitness and may develop into a lifetime leisure pursuit
- provides the chance for children of all abilities to experience movement in a different type of environment
- promotes the development of key water-safety skills
- assists with the delivery of other curriculum areas, especially science and personal, social and health education.

What to teach

Water confidence
Including getting in and out, resting and floating positions.

Water safety
Including being aware of hazards and basic survival skills.

Water games
Builds confidence and assists movement through the water.

Stroke technique
Including means of propulsion – arms and legs, front and back.

Some of the preparatory teaching in swimming can be done in the classroom, especially on aspects of health, hygiene and water safety. Safety issues that are particular to taking class swimming lessons are considered on page 13.

Schools can choose to teach swimming at Key Stage 1, although it is not a statutory requirement for that stage. If it is to be taught at Key Stage 1, children should be taught the Key Stage 2 programme of study at a level thought appropriate by the teacher.

Developing skills and understanding through themes

With the themes given in this section, it has been felt appropriate to show progression not according to age but according to experience. Water confidence, water safety and water games are therefore outlined from beginner through to proficient swimmer. Again this is only intended as a guide. Progression is not always linear and any child could be working on a number of different stages at any one time. The stroke technique theme follows a different format. Here progression shows how the stroke is introduced and developed in each swimming lesson. As with earlier photographs, the illustrations emphasise teaching points that can be made during the teaching of these themes.

Progression through Swimming

Makes an assisted entry into the water; helped down steps or from a sitting position on the side. →

Makes an unaided entry, choosing own ease-in gentle method.

↓

Moves across the pool in shallow water; plays face-wetting activities.

↓

Water confidence

Beginner

Holding poolside, in deeper water, lifts legs and makes a treading water action. ←

Floats in different ways, lifting legs and spreading the body – back down and face down. ←

Lifts legs off floor, pushes and glides from side and regains feet. Uses front and back in shallow water.

↓

Sculls with arm and legs while holding the side; conserves energy and makes a smooth action.

↓

Moves away from the side, treads water with a float, works on smooth leg actions.

↓

Treads water with no support and works on arm and leg action. →

Treads water wearing light clothing. →

Proficient swimmer

Water safety (personal survival)

Beginner

Is aware of rescue aids, what to use and items that float.

Knows the rules of cold water survival – keeping clothes on to retain body heat.

Knows how to behave near water (through class work), eg near the edge and not going alone.

Is aware of water hazards (through class work), warning signs and the dangers of swimming on a full stomach.

Knows where to get assistance – dialling 999.

Uses rescue aids at the poolside, eg ball, lifebelt, rubber ring and wood.

Uses aids to reach and pull people in, eg rope, towel and belt.

Is aware of individual survival techniques – uses float, shouts for help and adopts a position to retain heat.

Proficient swimmer

Takes a correctly-instructed course in life saving.

Is aware of group personal survival techniques – huddling together, using floating aids and keeping together.

A PRIMARY TEACHER'S HANDBOOK – *PE*

Water games

Beginner

Is aware of ways of travelling across the pool individually, eg walking hopping and bouncing.

Copies a partner or small group, eg raises arms or lifts legs off the floor.

Follows the leader across the water with tasks set, then changes over.

Plays tag-chasing games, children get caught by being touched.

Swims or walks across the pool, pushing a floating object, such as a ball, in front.

Blows a small floating object (eg a table tennis ball) across the surface of the pool, with the mouth near the water surface.

Plays a ball-passing game, such as mini-water polo in the deep end with targets to score.

Swims according to game rules, eg legs only or fewest strokes wins.

Picks up light objects from the bottom of a shallow pool.

Swims relays in small groups, climbing out of the water when finished.

Proficient swimmer

A PRIMARY TEACHER'S HANDBOOK – *PE*

Stroke technique

Start of lesson

Focuses on whole stroke, checks body position and picks items to work on.

Works with floats across widths, concentrating on leg action, using the side if necessary.

Warms up with rapid vigorous movements.

Revises recent work on stroke technique with brief recap of the previous lesson.

Works on arm action after watching a standing demonstration in shallow water.

Works on arm action while moving and co-ordinates with legs.

Tries whole strokes again and checks progression.

Knows how legs, arms, body, position and breathing fit in together.

Knows how to breathe and when to breathe while making the stroke.

Concluding activity – plays a water-based game with purpose to develop other skills, eg diving (provides a contrast with the rest of the lesson).

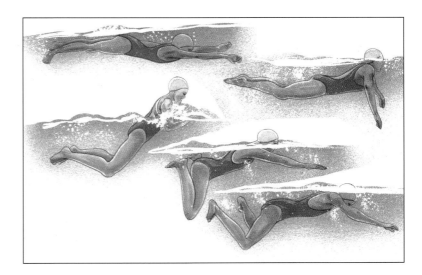

End of lesson

Assessing children's work in PE

Assessment provides evidence of individual progress and informs the teacher that objectives are being achieved. It needs to take place in planning, performing and evaluating. Assessment procedures should be used in conjunction with the National Curriculum End of Key Stage descriptions and any local authority guidelines. In PE it is particularly important to spend time assessing the children's capabilities and ability range when a new class is taken over.

Basic principles

Assessment should be:
- continuous and an integral part of normal teaching and learning
- flexible to suit the nature of the task being worked on
- related to the objectives and activities
- matched to the children's abilities
- based on recognised criteria including elements such as accuracy, adaptability and use of imagination
- organised to involve the child who should be encouraged to be self-critical
- used as a basis for future planning.

Methods to be used

Assess work through:
- **observing** – how the children plans, perform and evaluate their work
- **listening** – what the children say as they plan their work and reflect on what they have done
- **discussing** – with children as individuals or in groups as they think about their work
- **gathering** – using information that has been collected about children's performance in the past, eg recording
- **studying** – looking at written information children may have produced about their work
- **watching** – recording children's work on videotape for discussion and analysis later.

Types of assessment

Formative
This is an ongoing process that takes place during activity sessions and allows teachers to assess the child's current level of achievement.

Summative
This assesses overall achievement and comes at the end of a particular unit of work (see End of Key Stage descriptions as well).

Diagnostic
This type of assessment can be used to identify particular needs, strengths and weaknesses both individually and collectively.

Evaluate
This can be used to check how well progression is working and to influence future overall planning. (See page 61 for more details.)

Recording PE work

Class/teacher	Date	Time
Area of activity	Learning/teaching theme	

Learning targets	Equipment/apparatus	Layout/organisation

Opening activity (warm up)

Main activity (skill development/application)	Main teaching points

Concluding activity (cool down)

Assessment focus, skill or group, for the lesson	Comments/future planning

PE Record Sheet

Name				Class	

	Games	Gymnastics	Dance	Athletics	Swimming	Outdoor and adventurous activities
Skills development/ application						
Use of imagination						
Creativity						
Interpretation/ problem solving						
Working with others						
Health and safety						
Self-criticism/ evaluation						

Useful hints

- This is intended to be used for each child and filled in after lessons or as soon as possible thereafter.

- Choose to assess a small group of children or a single skill in a lesson.

- Link assessment to specific objectives and activities.

- Decide what to assess before the lesson.

- Child demonstrations will help evidence gathering.

- Remember to record evidence of planning, performing and evaluating.

This will assist with:
End of Key Stage descriptions.
Reporting to parents.
Information for new teachers.

A PRIMARY TEACHER'S HANDBOOK – PE

Evaluating the PE lesson

Things to think about

- Keep evaluation targets realistic and manageable.
- Concentrate on different aspects in different lessons.
- Focus on one or two questions in a lesson.

Organisation

- Did signals and instructions get immediate response?
- Were you as the teacher well positioned to see the class?
- Was the use of the voice varied?
- Were demonstrations clearly seen?
- Were noise levels satisfactory?
- Was observation put to good use?
- Was enough time allowed for each part of the lesson?
- Did group activities work well?
- Could groups be organised before the lesson?
- Did changing sessions run smoothly?

Teaching and learning targets

- Was the lesson structured to permit a build up in skills?
- Were the objectives of the lesson achieved?
- Did learning outcomes match intentions?
- What effort was made to differentiate by task and not outcome?
- Was appropriate feedback given?
- Did tasks match ability level?
- Were teaching points used effectively?
- Was there evidence of progression?
- Did the children have a chance to discuss their work?
- Was there time to reflect and evaluate?
- Was there a good balance between teaching and time to explore?

THE TEACHER

Equipment and apparatus

- Was equipment ready to use?
- Was the right equipment chosen?
- Was there easy access to equipment?
- Was equipment placed in safe areas?
- Was equipment handled and moved safely?
- Was equipment used safely?
- Was equipment fully exploited?
- Was equipment checked before being returned?
- Were any gaps in equipment noted?

Health and safety

- Was available space used to best advantage?
- Were there near misses or collisions – why did they happen and how could they be prevented?
- Was there rigorous physical activity?
- Did the children work hard?
- Did the children enjoy themselves?
- Were the children dressed correctly?
- Did the children learn more about the benefits of exercise?
- Did the children learn more about the use and control of their bodies?
- Did the children learn more about health, safety and hygiene?

Use the results of these evaluations to help monitor that progression is taking place and to 'feed forward' for future planning.

Resources

Useful work areas markings

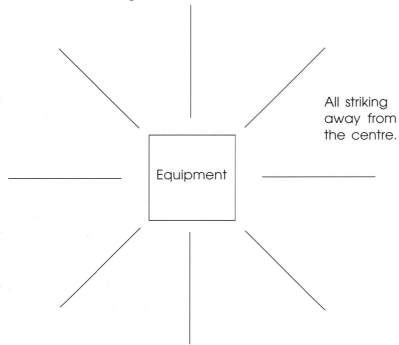

All striking away from the centre.

Equipment

This star arrangement is useful for striking and fielding games. Equipment is based in the centre and the teacher patrols around the outside. The children take part in small games with their backs to the equipment, striking the same way. Star lines should be 15–20m long.

This box grid system is very useful for mini versions of invasion games. It could also be used by groups for net and racket activities. Use 8m boxes for younger children and up to 10m for those who are older.

Make smaller working areas for games activities by using ropes, cones, flags, skittles and beanbags to subdivide larger areas such as football pitches and netball courts. Supplies of playground chalk can also be put to good use.

Some useful addresses

The Royal Life Saving Society UK,
Mountbatten House,
Studley,
Warwickshire
B80 7NN
Tel: 01527 853943

The British Orienteering Federation,
Riversdale,
Dale Road North,
Darly Dale,
Matlock,
Derbyshire
DE4 2HX
Tel: 01629 734042

Amateur Swimming Association,
Harold Fern House,
Derby Square,
Loughborough
LE11 0AL
Tel: 01509 230431

British Athletics,
225a Bristol Road,
Edgbaston,
Birmingham
B5 7UB
Tel: 0121 4405000

British Amateur Gymnastics,
Ford Hall,
Lilleshaw National Sports Centre,
Newport,
Shropshire
TF10 9NB
Tel: 01952 820330

National Resource Centre for Dance,
University of Surrey,
Guildford,
Surrey
GU2 5XH
Tel: 01483 259316

This type of letter could be used when an off-site visit has been arranged as part of the Outdoor and adventurous activities programme. It is intended as a guide only.

Name and address
of school

Date

Use a heading to give the activity a title, eg Class 3D visit to Woodland Park

Dear Parent/Guardian/Carer,

As part of the work the children in Class 3D are doing in the Outdoor and adventurous activities section of the PE curriculum, a visit has been arranged to Woodland Park.

This will take place on March 14th. The children will leave the school at 1.30pm and return in time for the end of school at 3.30pm. If the weather is very wet, the visit will take place on March 15th.

During the visit the children will be walking several trails in the park and will be stopping at various points to discuss and make notes on what they have seen. The visit will be followed up in the classroom later.

Staff would be grateful if you could ensure the children are suitably clothed. They will need warm, waterproof coats, preferably with hoods, and should wear wellington boots or strong walking shoes.

Members of staff will be accompanying the children so there will be adequate supervision, but we would welcome support from any parents who are available to join us on the visit.

Please complete, detach and return the form at the bottom of this letter as soon as possible, indicating that you give permission for your child to go. Please also indicate if you are able to come yourself. We shall walk the short distance from the school to the Park and no cost will be involved.

Yours sincerely

- -

I agree that my child _____ is able to go on the visit to Woodland Park on March 14th or 15th.
I am/am not able to come as a parent helper for the visit.

Signed _____ Date _____

End matters

Physical Education and Sport

With much written and spoken in the highest quarters about the importance of sport in the life of primary school children, some distinction needs to be made clear in school policy documents and schemes of work between PE and sport.

A recent National Curriculum document (PE in the National Curriculum, DES, April 1992, Page H1) illustrated the essential difference between the two. PE was defined as '... learning in a mainly physical context. The purpose of the learning is to develop specific knowledge, skills and understanding ...'. Sport on the other hand was defined as '... a range of physical activities where emphasis is on participation and competition'. With this in mind, it seems appropriate that the correct vehicle for the delivery of National Curriculum PE to all the children in the class is the class-based PE lesson, while sport is dealt with for those who are interested in extra-curricular clubs and activities.

Award schemes

A whole range of awards, badges and certificates are available in many areas of PE, notably swimming, athletics and gymnastic activities. At one end these encourage beginners to achieve their first steps in a particular skill and at the other they reward high levels of competence. It is important to remember, however, that awards should be seen as a natural consequence of a structured teaching programme and should not themselves drive the PE curriculum.

Sports day and swimming galas

These continue to remain key events in the primary school calendar. While the accent will be on children competing against their own best performance or against other children, it should not be a case of winning or achieving at all costs. All children should be encouraged to take part unless there are special reasons why they are not able to do so. The range of events organised should allow all children to achieve some measure of success, either in a team, a group or as an individual. Events should aim to cater for all skill levels.

Postscript

While primary school teachers always seek to lay the foundations for lifelong interest in all curriculum areas, children who come to find enjoyment and satisfaction in PE will not only find it life enriching, but also possibly life saving and life prolonging.